THE
BOOKISH
SLEUTH

Mystery Reader's

JOURNAL AND PLANNER

(2022)

THE BOOKISH SLEUTH
Mystery Reader's Journal and Planner (2022)
Published by McGuffin Ink

ISBN: 978-1-950054-46-6

Cover and interior design by Qamber Designs and Media

Dear Mystery Reader,

Some readers record the books they read in a meticulous fashion. I have never been one of those people—until recently.

I've always moved from book to book with only a vague system to track my reading. As my GoodReads and Library Thing shelves attest, I tried various online systems, but my logins became sporadic and my usage spotty until it tapered off completely. There were just too many new books calling to me, and I didn't take the time to jot down details about the books or my thoughts on the mystery once I'd finished (or abandoned!) them.

But then I started Mystery Books Podcast, a podcast devoted to helping readers discover new books to read. My rather haphazard system of keeping track of my mystery books didn't work. I need a way to help me remember all the details about the books—characters, tone, fun quotes, and the mystery elements—so that I could discuss the book months later when I recorded episodes.

I tried various print journals, but none of them were quite what I needed. None of them had a way to keep track of the mystery aspects of the books, such as suspects, clues, and red herrings, plus a whole host of other items I wanted to jot down.

In December of 2020, I bought a new calendar and was writing down various bookish days that I wanted to keep track of in 2021, when a thought hit me: what if I combined a calendar and a reading journal for mystery readers? I could include all my favorite bookish dates, and I could also create a journal to help me remember all the details I need to know for my podcast.

I surveyed my readers and they were enthusiastic about the idea. They also provided plenty of new ideas to include like the yearly reading tracker and pages to list series to read.

The Bookish Sleuth began as an idea that would meet a need I had, but it's turned into something very special to me. It's the result of brainstorming with my readers and a wonderful collaboration with my designers, who created the gorgeous interior and cover.

I hope you enjoy using the The Bookish Sleuth. I wish you many hours of bookish escapes!

Happy sleuthing,

Sara

Table of Contents

YEARLY *Book Tracker*

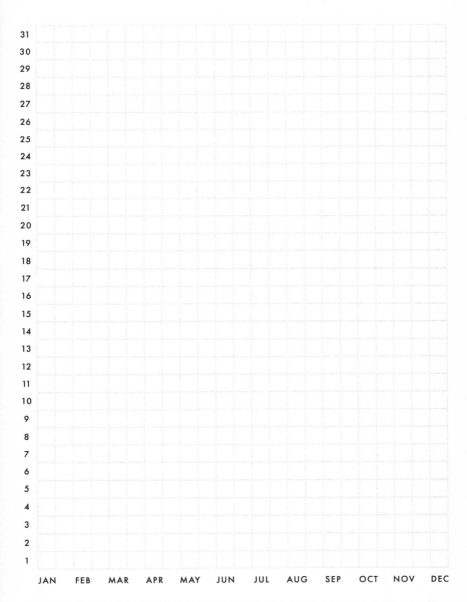

	JAN	FEB	MAR	APR	MAY	JUN	JUL	AUG	SEP	OCT	NOV	DEC
31												
30												
29												
28												
27												
26												
25												
24												
23												
22												
21												
20												
19												
18												
17												
16												
15												
14												
13												
12												
11												
10												
9												
8												
7												
6												
5												
4												
3												
2												
1												

COLOR/SHADE IN EACH SQUARE WITH EVERY BOOK YOU FINISHED THAT MONTH

Books to Read

TITLE	AUTHOR

Series to Read

SERIES	TITLE	AUTHOR

Wishlist

Recommended List

BOOK TITLE / AUTHOR	RECOMMENDED TO	WHY

DNF (DID NOT FINISH) LIST

BOOK TITLE / AUTHOR	BOOK TITLE / AUTHOR

January

"Another dead body.
Every year it is the same. Every year,
another dead body . . ."

Lion in the Valley by Elizabeth Peters

January

SUNDAY	MONDAY	TUESDAY	WEDNESDAY
30	31		
2	3	4	5
9	10	11	12
16	17	18	19
23	24	25	26

BOOKISH DATES OF THE MONTH

5 - Umberto Eco's birthday

6 - Joan Hess' birthday

18 - Thesaurus Day

19 - Edgar Allan Poe's birthday

26 - Library Shelfie Day

THURSDAY	FRIDAY	SATURDAY
		1
6	7	8
13	14	15
20	21	22
27	28	29

BOOK TITLE [   ]   AUTHOR [   ]

GENRE   SERIES   SERIES #   PAGE COUNT/HOURS
[   ]   [   ]   [   ]   [   ]

FORMAT:
EBOOK | PAPERBACK | AUDIOBOOK
LIBRARY BORROW | KINDLE UNLIMITED | OTHER

RATING ☆☆☆☆☆

DATE STARTED   DATE FINISHED
[   ]   [   ]   DID NOT FINISH [   ]

MAIN CHARACTER(S) [   ]

SUPPORTING CHARACTERS [   ]

SETTING [   ]

WHODUNIT [   ]

THOUGHTS ON THE PLOT/THEME

THOUGHTS ON MYSTERY

THOUGHTS ON CHARACTERS

Wrap up Section

WHY I READ THIS BOOK

FAVORITE QUOTES

THINGS I LIKED

THINGS I DIDN'T LIKE

RECOMMEND THIS TO

TAGS/CATEGORY
(PLACE TO NOTE GOODREADS SHELF
OR BLOG POST CATEGORY)

FEELING, MOOD, TONE

BOOK TITLE [   ] AUTHOR [   ]

GENRE   SERIES   SERIES #   PAGE COUNT/HOURS
[   ]   [   ]   [   ]   [   ]

FORMAT:
EBOOK | PAPERBACK | AUDIOBOOK
LIBRARY BORROW | KINDLE UNLIMITED | OTHER

RATING ☆☆☆☆☆

DATE STARTED   DATE FINISHED
[   ]   [   ]   DID NOT FINISH [ ]

MAIN CHARACTER(S) [   ]

SUPPORTING CHARACTERS [   ]

SETTING [   ]

WHODUNIT [   ]

THOUGHTS ON THE PLOT/THEME

THOUGHTS ON MYSTERY

THOUGHTS ON CHARACTERS

Wrap up Section

WHY I READ THIS BOOK

FAVORITE QUOTES

THINGS I LIKED

THINGS I DIDN'T LIKE

RECOMMEND THIS TO

TAGS/CATEGORY
(PLACE TO NOTE GOODREADS SHELF
OR BLOG POST CATEGORY)

FEELING, MOOD, TONE 😃 😌 😍 😣 😂 😲

BOOK TITLE [   ] AUTHOR [   ]

GENRE   SERIES   SERIES # PAGE COUNT/HOURS
[   ]   [   ]   [   ]   [   ]

FORMAT:

EBOOK | PAPERBACK | AUDIOBOOK
LIBRARY BORROW | KINDLE UNLIMITED | OTHER

RATING ☆☆☆☆☆

DATE STARTED   DATE FINISHED
[   ]   [   ]   DID NOT FINISH [ ]

MAIN CHARACTER(S) [   ]

SUPPORTING CHARACTERS [   ]

SETTING [   ]

WHODUNIT [   ]

THOUGHTS ON THE PLOT/THEME

THOUGHTS ON MYSTERY

THOUGHTS ON CHARACTERS

Wrap up Section

WHY I READ THIS BOOK

FAVORITE QUOTES

THINGS I LIKED

THINGS I DIDN'T LIKE

RECOMMEND THIS TO

TAGS/CATEGORY
(PLACE TO NOTE GOODREADS SHELF
OR BLOG POST CATEGORY)

FEELING, MOOD, TONE

BOOK TITLE [   ]   **AUTHOR** [   ]

GENRE   **SERIES**   **SERIES #**   **PAGE COUNT/HOURS**
[   ]   [   ]   [   ]   [   ]

FORMAT:
EBOOK | PAPERBACK | AUDIOBOOK
LIBRARY BORROW | KINDLE UNLIMITED | OTHER

RATING ☆☆☆☆☆

DATE STARTED   **DATE FINISHED**
[   ]   [   ]   **DID NOT FINISH** [   ]

MAIN CHARACTER(S) [   ]

SUPPORTING CHARACTERS [   ]

SETTING [   ]

WHODUNIT [   ]

THOUGHTS ON THE PLOT/THEME

THOUGHTS ON MYSTERY

THOUGHTS ON CHARACTERS

Wrap up Section

WHY I READ THIS BOOK

FAVORITE QUOTES

THINGS I LIKED

THINGS I DIDN'T LIKE

RECOMMEND THIS TO

TAGS/CATEGORY
(PLACE TO NOTE GOODREADS SHELF
OR BLOG POST CATEGORY)

FEELING, MOOD, TONE 😃 😔 😍 😥 😂 😯

BOOK TITLE [   ]   AUTHOR [   ]

GENRE   SERIES   SERIES #   PAGE COUNT/HOURS
[   ]   [   ]   [   ]   [   ]

FORMAT:
EBOOK | PAPERBACK | AUDIOBOOK
LIBRARY BORROW | KINDLE UNLIMITED | OTHER

RATING ☆☆☆☆☆

DATE STARTED   DATE FINISHED
[   ]   [   ]   DID NOT FINISH [ ]

MAIN CHARACTER(S) [   ]

SUPPORTING CHARACTERS [   ]

SETTING [   ]

WHODUNIT [   ]

THOUGHTS ON THE PLOT/THEME

THOUGHTS ON MYSTERY

THOUGHTS ON CHARACTERS

30

Wrap up Section

WHY I READ THIS BOOK

FAVORITE QUOTES

THINGS I LIKED

THINGS I DIDN'T LIKE

RECOMMEND THIS TO

TAGS/CATEGORY
{PLACE TO NOTE GOODREADS SHELF
OR BLOG POST CATEGORY}

FEELING, MOOD, TONE

February

"There is nothing more deceptive than an obvious fact."
The Adventures of Sherlock Holmes by Arthur Conan Doyle

February

Love Your Library Month

SUNDAY	MONDAY	TUESDAY	WEDNESDAY
		1	2
6	7	8	9
13	14	15	16
20	21	22	23
27	28		

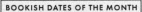

BOOKISH DATES OF THE MONTH

2 - World Read Aloud Day
14 - Library Lover's Day
15 - Anthony Gilbert's birthday
17 - Ruth Rendell's birthday

THURSDAY	FRIDAY	SATURDAY
3	4	5
10	11	12
17	18	19
24	25	26

BOOK TITLE [   ]   AUTHOR [   ]

GENRE   SERIES   SERIES #   PAGE COUNT/HOURS
[   ]   [   ]   [   ]   [   ]

FORMAT:
EBOOK | PAPERBACK | AUDIOBOOK
LIBRARY BORROW | KINDLE UNLIMITED | OTHER

RATING ☆☆☆☆☆

DATE STARTED   DATE FINISHED
[   ]   [   ]   DID NOT FINISH [ ]

MAIN CHARACTER(S) [   ]

SUPPORTING CHARACTERS [   ]

SETTING [   ]

WHODUNIT [   ]

THOUGHTS ON THE PLOT/THEME

THOUGHTS ON MYSTERY

THOUGHTS ON CHARACTERS

Wrap up Section

WHY I READ THIS BOOK

FAVORITE QUOTES

THINGS I LIKED

THINGS I DIDN'T LIKE

RECOMMEND THIS TO

TAGS/CATEGORY
(PLACE TO NOTE GOODREADS SHELF
OR BLOG POST CATEGORY)

FEELING, MOOD, TONE

BOOK TITLE [   ]   AUTHOR [   ]

GENRE   SERIES   SERIES #   PAGE COUNT/HOURS
[   ]   [   ]   [   ]   [   ]

FORMAT:

EBOOK | PAPERBACK | AUDIOBOOK
LIBRARY BORROW | KINDLE UNLIMITED | OTHER

RATING ☆☆☆☆☆

DATE STARTED   DATE FINISHED
[   ]   [   ]   DID NOT FINISH [ ]

MAIN CHARACTER(S) [   ]

SUPPORTING CHARACTERS [   ]

SETTING [   ]

WHODUNIT [   ]

THOUGHTS ON THE PLOT/THEME

THOUGHTS ON MYSTERY

THOUGHTS ON CHARACTERS

Wrap up Section

WHY I READ THIS BOOK

FAVORITE QUOTES

THINGS I LIKED

THINGS I DIDN'T LIKE

RECOMMEND THIS TO

TAGS/CATEGORY
(PLACE TO NOTE GOODREADS SHELF
OR BLOG POST CATEGORY)

FEELING, MOOD, TONE

BOOK TITLE [   ]   AUTHOR [   ]

GENRE   SERIES   SERIES #   PAGE COUNT/HOURS
[   ]   [   ]   [   ]   [   ]

FORMAT:
EBOOK | PAPERBACK | AUDIOBOOK   RATING ☆☆☆☆☆
LIBRARY BORROW | KINDLE UNLIMITED | OTHER

DATE STARTED   DATE FINISHED
[   ]   [   ]   DID NOT FINISH [ ]

MAIN CHARACTER(S) [   ]

SUPPORTING CHARACTERS [   ]

SETTING [   ]

WHODUNIT [   ]

THOUGHTS ON THE PLOT/THEME

THOUGHTS ON MYSTERY

THOUGHTS ON CHARACTERS

Wrap up Section

WHY I READ THIS BOOK

FAVORITE QUOTES

THINGS I LIKED

THINGS I DIDN'T LIKE

RECOMMEND THIS TO

TAGS/CATEGORY
(PLACE TO NOTE GOODREADS SHELF
OR BLOG POST CATEGORY)

FEELING, MOOD, TONE

BOOK TITLE [   ] AUTHOR [   ]

GENRE   SERIES   SERIES #   PAGE COUNT/HOURS
[   ]   [   ]   [   ]   [   ]

FORMAT:
EBOOK | PAPERBACK | AUDIOBOOK   RATING ☆☆☆☆☆
LIBRARY BORROW | KINDLE UNLIMITED | OTHER

DATE STARTED   DATE FINISHED
[   ]   [   ]   DID NOT FINISH [ ]

MAIN CHARACTER(S) [   ]

SUPPORTING CHARACTERS [   ]

SETTING [   ]

WHODUNIT [   ]

THOUGHTS ON THE PLOT/THEME

THOUGHTS ON MYSTERY

THOUGHTS ON CHARACTERS

Wrap up Section

WHY I READ THIS BOOK

FAVORITE QUOTES

THINGS I LIKED

THINGS I DIDN'T LIKE

RECOMMEND THIS TO

TAGS/CATEGORY
{PLACE TO NOTE GOODREADS SHELF
OR BLOG POST CATEGORY}

FEELING, MOOD, TONE 😃 😌 😍 😟 😂 😲

BOOK TITLE [   ]   AUTHOR [   ]

GENRE   SERIES   SERIES #   PAGE COUNT/HOURS
[   ]   [   ]   [   ]   [   ]

FORMAT:
EBOOK | PAPERBACK | AUDIOBOOK
LIBRARY BORROW | KINDLE UNLIMITED | OTHER

RATING ☆☆☆☆☆

DATE STARTED   DATE FINISHED
[   ]   [   ]   DID NOT FINISH [ ]

MAIN CHARACTER(S) [   ]

SUPPORTING CHARACTERS [   ]

SETTING [   ]

WHODUNIT [   ]

THOUGHTS ON THE PLOT/THEME

THOUGHTS ON MYSTERY

THOUGHTS ON CHARACTERS

Wrap up Section

WHY I READ THIS BOOK

FAVORITE QUOTES

THINGS I LIKED

THINGS I DIDN'T LIKE

RECOMMEND THIS TO

TAGS/CATEGORY
(PLACE TO NOTE GOODREADS SHELF
OR BLOG POST CATEGORY)

FEELING, MOOD, TONE

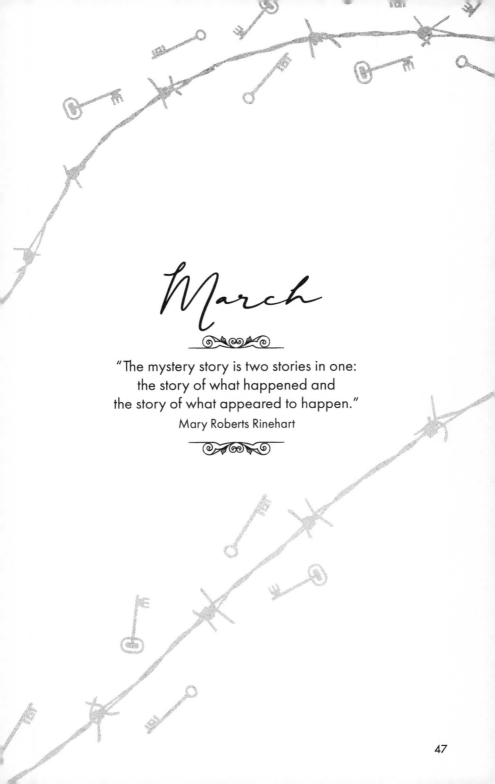

March

"The mystery story is two stories in one:
the story of what happened and
the story of what appeared to happen."

Mary Roberts Rinehart

March

First full week of March - Read an eBook Week

SUNDAY	MONDAY	TUESDAY	WEDNESDAY
		1	2
6	7	8	9
13	14	15	16
20	21	22	23
27	28	29	30

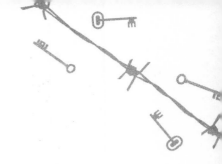

THURSDAY	FRIDAY	SATURDAY
3	4	5
10	11	12
17	18	19
24	25	26
31		

BOOK TITLE [＿＿＿＿＿＿＿＿＿] AUTHOR [＿＿＿＿＿＿＿]

GENRE   SERIES   SERIES #   PAGE COUNT/HOURS
[＿＿＿＿＿]   [＿＿＿＿＿＿]   [＿＿]   [＿＿＿＿＿＿＿]

FORMAT:
EBOOK | PAPERBACK | AUDIOBOOK   RATING ☆☆☆☆☆
LIBRARY BORROW | KINDLE UNLIMITED | OTHER

DATE STARTED   DATE FINISHED
[＿＿＿＿＿＿]   [＿＿＿＿＿＿]   DID NOT FINISH [＿]

MAIN CHARACTER(S) [＿＿＿＿＿＿＿＿＿＿＿＿＿＿＿]

SUPPORTING CHARACTERS [＿＿＿＿＿＿＿＿＿＿＿]

SETTING [＿＿＿＿＿＿＿＿＿＿＿＿＿＿＿＿＿]

WHODUNIT [＿＿＿＿＿＿＿＿＿＿＿＿＿＿＿]

THOUGHTS ON THE PLOT/THEME

THOUGHTS ON MYSTERY

THOUGHTS ON CHARACTERS

Wrap up Section

WHY I READ THIS BOOK

FAVORITE QUOTES

THINGS I LIKED

THINGS I DIDN'T LIKE

RECOMMEND THIS TO

TAGS/CATEGORY
(PLACE TO NOTE GOODREADS SHELF
OR BLOG POST CATEGORY)

FEELING, MOOD, TONE

BOOK TITLE [   ]   AUTHOR [   ]

GENRE   SERIES   SERIES #   PAGE COUNT/HOURS
[   ]   [   ]   [   ]   [   ]

FORMAT:

EBOOK | PAPERBACK | AUDIOBOOK
LIBRARY BORROW | KINDLE UNLIMITED | OTHER

RATING ☆☆☆☆☆

DATE STARTED   DATE FINISHED
[   ]   [   ]   DID NOT FINISH [   ]

MAIN CHARACTER(S) [   ]

SUPPORTING CHARACTERS [   ]

SETTING [   ]

WHODUNIT [   ]

THOUGHTS ON THE PLOT/THEME

THOUGHTS ON MYSTERY

THOUGHTS ON CHARACTERS

Wrap up Section

WHY I READ THIS BOOK

FAVORITE QUOTES

THINGS I LIKED

THINGS I DIDN'T LIKE

RECOMMEND THIS TO

TAGS/CATEGORY
(PLACE TO NOTE GOODREADS SHELF
OR BLOG POST CATEGORY)

FEELING, MOOD, TONE

BOOK TITLE [   ]   AUTHOR [   ]

GENRE   SERIES   SERIES #   PAGE COUNT/HOURS
[   ]   [   ]   [   ]   [   ]

FORMAT:
EBOOK | PAPERBACK | AUDIOBOOK
LIBRARY BORROW | KINDLE UNLIMITED | OTHER

RATING ☆☆☆☆☆

DATE STARTED   DATE FINISHED
[   ]   [   ]   DID NOT FINISH [ ]

MAIN CHARACTER(S) [   ]

SUPPORTING CHARACTERS [   ]

SETTING [   ]

WHODUNIT [   ]

THOUGHTS ON THE PLOT/THEME

THOUGHTS ON MYSTERY

THOUGHTS ON CHARACTERS

Wrap up Section

WHY I READ THIS BOOK

FAVORITE QUOTES

THINGS I LIKED

THINGS I DIDN'T LIKE

RECOMMEND THIS TO

TAGS/CATEGORY
{PLACE TO NOTE GOODREADS SHELF
OR BLOG POST CATEGORY}

FEELING, MOOD, TONE 😃 😌 😍 😣 😂 😮

BOOK TITLE [   ]   AUTHOR [   ]

GENRE   SERIES   SERIES #   PAGE COUNT/HOURS
[   ]   [   ]   [   ]   [   ]

FORMAT:
EBOOK | PAPERBACK | AUDIOBOOK   RATING ☆☆☆☆☆
LIBRARY BORROW | KINDLE UNLIMITED | OTHER

DATE STARTED   DATE FINISHED
[   ]   [   ]   DID NOT FINISH [ ]

MAIN CHARACTER(S) [   ]

SUPPORTING CHARACTERS [   ]

SETTING [   ]

WHODUNIT [   ]

THOUGHTS ON THE PLOT/THEME

THOUGHTS ON MYSTERY

THOUGHTS ON CHARACTERS

Wrap up Section

WHY I READ THIS BOOK

FAVORITE QUOTES

THINGS I LIKED

THINGS I DIDN'T LIKE

RECOMMEND THIS TO

TAGS/CATEGORY
(PLACE TO NOTE GOODREADS SHELF
OR BLOG POST CATEGORY)

FEELING, MOOD, TONE

BOOK TITLE [   ] AUTHOR [   ]

GENRE   SERIES   SERIES #   PAGE COUNT/HOURS
[   ]   [   ]   [   ]   [   ]

FORMAT:
EBOOK | PAPERBACK | AUDIOBOOK
LIBRARY BORROW | KINDLE UNLIMITED | OTHER

RATING ☆☆☆☆☆

DATE STARTED   DATE FINISHED
[   ]   [   ]   DID NOT FINISH [ ]

MAIN CHARACTER(S) [   ]

SUPPORTING CHARACTERS [   ]

SETTING [   ]

WHODUNIT [   ]

THOUGHTS ON THE PLOT/THEME

THOUGHTS ON MYSTERY

THOUGHTS ON CHARACTERS

Wrap up Section

WHY I READ THIS BOOK

FAVORITE QUOTES

THINGS I LIKED

THINGS I DIDN'T LIKE

RECOMMEND THIS TO

TAGS/CATEGORY
{PLACE TO NOTE GOODREADS SHELF
OR BLOG POST CATEGORY}

FEELING, MOOD, TONE

April

"All things are poisons, for there is nothing
without poisonous qualities.
It is only the dose which makes a thing poison."

Paracelsus

SUNDAY	MONDAY	TUESDAY	WEDNESDAY
3	4	5	6
10	11	12	13
17	18	19	20
24	25	26	27

BOOKISH DATES OF THE MONTH

5 - Anthony Horowitz's birthday
16 - National Librarian's Day
21 - Gladys Mitchell's birthday
23 - World Book Day
23 - Ngaio Marsh's birthday
24 - Sue Grafton's birthday
28 - Ian Rankin's birthday
30 - Independent Bookstore Day

THURSDAY	FRIDAY	SATURDAY
	1	2
7	8	9
14	15	16
21	22	23
28	29	30

BOOK TITLE [   ] AUTHOR [   ]

GENRE   SERIES   SERIES #   PAGE COUNT/HOURS
[   ]   [   ]   [   ]   [   ]

FORMAT:
EBOOK | PAPERBACK | AUDIOBOOK
LIBRARY BORROW | KINDLE UNLIMITED | OTHER

RATING ☆☆☆☆☆

DATE STARTED   DATE FINISHED
[   ]   [   ]   DID NOT FINISH [ ]

MAIN CHARACTER(S) [   ]

SUPPORTING CHARACTERS [   ]

SETTING [   ]

WHODUNIT [   ]

THOUGHTS ON THE PLOT/THEME

THOUGHTS ON MYSTERY

THOUGHTS ON CHARACTERS

Wrap up Section

WHY I READ THIS BOOK

FAVORITE QUOTES

THINGS I LIKED

THINGS I DIDN'T LIKE

RECOMMEND THIS TO

TAGS/CATEGORY
(PLACE TO NOTE GOODREADS SHELF
OR BLOG POST CATEGORY)

FEELING, MOOD, TONE 😃 😔 😍 😥 😂 😲

BOOK TITLE [   ]   AUTHOR [   ]

GENRE   SERIES   SERIES #   PAGE COUNT/HOURS
[   ]   [   ]   [   ]   [   ]

FORMAT:
EBOOK | PAPERBACK | AUDIOBOOK
LIBRARY BORROW | KINDLE UNLIMITED | OTHER

RATING ☆☆☆☆☆

DATE STARTED   DATE FINISHED
[   ]   [   ]   DID NOT FINISH [   ]

MAIN CHARACTER(S) [   ]

SUPPORTING CHARACTERS [   ]

SETTING [   ]

WHODUNIT [   ]

THOUGHTS ON THE PLOT/THEME

THOUGHTS ON MYSTERY

THOUGHTS ON CHARACTERS

Wrap up Section

WHY I READ THIS BOOK

FAVORITE QUOTES

THINGS I LIKED

THINGS I DIDN'T LIKE

RECOMMEND THIS TO

TAGS/CATEGORY
(PLACE TO NOTE GOODREADS SHELF
OR BLOG POST CATEGORY)

FEELING, MOOD, TONE 😃 😔 😍 😢 😆 😲

BOOK TITLE [   ]   AUTHOR [   ]

GENRE   SERIES   SERIES #   PAGE COUNT/HOURS
[   ]   [   ]   [   ]   [   ]

FORMAT:

EBOOK | PAPERBACK | AUDIOBOOK
LIBRARY BORROW | KINDLE UNLIMITED | OTHER

RATING ☆☆☆☆☆

DATE STARTED   DATE FINISHED
[   ]   [   ]   DID NOT FINISH [ ]

MAIN CHARACTER(S) [   ]

SUPPORTING CHARACTERS [   ]

SETTING [   ]

WHODUNIT [   ]

THOUGHTS ON THE PLOT/THEME

THOUGHTS ON MYSTERY

THOUGHTS ON CHARACTERS

Wrap up Section

WHY I READ THIS BOOK

FAVORITE QUOTES

THINGS I LIKED

THINGS I DIDN'T LIKE

RECOMMEND THIS TO

TAGS/CATEGORY
(PLACE TO NOTE GOODREADS SHELF
OR BLOG POST CATEGORY)

FEELING, MOOD, TONE 😃 😌 😍 😥 😂 😲

BOOK TITLE [   ]   AUTHOR [   ]

GENRE   SERIES   SERIES #   PAGE COUNT/HOURS
[   ]   [   ]   [   ]   [   ]

FORMAT:
EBOOK | PAPERBACK | AUDIOBOOK
LIBRARY BORROW | KINDLE UNLIMITED | OTHER

RATING ☆☆☆☆☆

DATE STARTED   DATE FINISHED
[   ]   [   ]   DID NOT FINISH [   ]

MAIN CHARACTER(S) [   ]
SUPPORTING CHARACTERS [   ]
SETTING [   ]
WHODUNIT [   ]

THOUGHTS ON THE PLOT/THEME

THOUGHTS ON MYSTERY

THOUGHTS ON CHARACTERS

Wrap up Section

WHY I READ THIS BOOK

FAVORITE QUOTES

THINGS I LIKED

THINGS I DIDN'T LIKE

RECOMMEND THIS TO

TAGS/CATEGORY
(PLACE TO NOTE GOODREADS SHELF
OR BLOG POST CATEGORY)

FEELING, MOOD, TONE 😃 😌 😍 🥺 😂 😲

BOOK TITLE [ ] **AUTHOR** [ ]

GENRE [ ] **SERIES** [ ] **SERIES #** [ ] **PAGE COUNT/HOURS** [ ]

FORMAT:

EBOOK | PAPERBACK | AUDIOBOOK
LIBRARY BORROW | KINDLE UNLIMITED | OTHER

RATING ☆☆☆☆☆

DATE STARTED [ ] **DATE FINISHED** [ ] **DID NOT FINISH** [ ]

MAIN CHARACTER(S) [ ]

SUPPORTING CHARACTERS [ ]

SETTING [ ]

WHODUNIT [ ]

THOUGHTS ON THE PLOT/THEME

THOUGHTS ON MYSTERY

THOUGHTS ON CHARACTERS

Wrap up Section

WHY I READ THIS BOOK

FAVORITE QUOTES

THINGS I LIKED

THINGS I DIDN'T LIKE

RECOMMEND THIS TO

TAGS/CATEGORY
(PLACE TO NOTE GOODREADS SHELF
OR BLOG POST CATEGORY)

FEELING, MOOD, TONE

May

The best crime novels are all based
on people keeping secrets.

Alafair Burke

May

Mystery Month and Get Caught Reading Month

SUNDAY	MONDAY	TUESDAY	WEDNESDAY
1	2	3	4
8	9	10	11
15	16	17	18
22	23	24	25
29	30	31	

THURSDAY	FRIDAY	SATURDAY
5	6	7
12	13	14
19	20	21
26	27	28

BOOK TITLE _____ AUTHOR _____

GENRE   SERIES   SERIES #   PAGE COUNT/HOURS
_____   _____   _____   _____

FORMAT:
EBOOK | PAPERBACK | AUDIOBOOK
LIBRARY BORROW | KINDLE UNLIMITED | OTHER

RATING ☆☆☆☆☆

DATE STARTED   DATE FINISHED
_____ _____   DID NOT FINISH _____

MAIN CHARACTER(S) _____

SUPPORTING CHARACTERS _____

SETTING _____

WHODUNIT _____

THOUGHTS ON THE PLOT/THEME

THOUGHTS ON MYSTERY

THOUGHTS ON CHARACTERS

Wrap up Section

WHY I READ THIS BOOK

FAVORITE QUOTES

THINGS I LIKED

THINGS I DIDN'T LIKE

RECOMMEND THIS TO

TAGS/CATEGORY
(PLACE TO NOTE GOODREADS SHELF
OR BLOG POST CATEGORY)

FEELING, MOOD, TONE 😃 😔 😍 😟 😂 😲

BOOK TITLE [   ]   AUTHOR [   ]

GENRE   SERIES   SERIES #   PAGE COUNT/HOURS
[   ]   [   ]   [   ]   [   ]

FORMAT:

EBOOK | PAPERBACK | AUDIOBOOK
LIBRARY BORROW | KINDLE UNLIMITED | OTHER

RATING ☆☆☆☆☆

DATE STARTED   DATE FINISHED
[   ]   [   ]   DID NOT FINISH [ ]

MAIN CHARACTER(S) [   ]

SUPPORTING CHARACTERS [   ]

SETTING [   ]

WHODUNIT [   ]

THOUGHTS ON THE PLOT/THEME

THOUGHTS ON MYSTERY

THOUGHTS ON CHARACTERS

Wrap up Section

WHY I READ THIS BOOK

FAVORITE QUOTES

THINGS I LIKED

THINGS I DIDN'T LIKE

RECOMMEND THIS TO

TAGS/CATEGORY
(PLACE TO NOTE GOODREADS SHELF
OR BLOG POST CATEGORY)

FEELING, MOOD, TONE 😃 😔 😍 🥺 😂 😲

BOOK TITLE [   ]   AUTHOR [   ]

GENRE   SERIES   SERIES #   PAGE COUNT/HOURS
[   ]   [   ]   [   ]   [   ]

FORMAT:
EBOOK | PAPERBACK | AUDIOBOOK
LIBRARY BORROW | KINDLE UNLIMITED | OTHER

RATING ☆☆☆☆☆

DATE STARTED   DATE FINISHED
[   ]   [   ]   DID NOT FINISH [ ]

MAIN CHARACTER(S) [   ]

SUPPORTING CHARACTERS [   ]

SETTING [   ]

WHODUNIT [   ]

🌿 THOUGHTS ON THE PLOT/THEME 🌿

🌿 THOUGHTS ON MYSTERY 🌿

🌿 THOUGHTS ON CHARACTERS 🌿

Wrap up Section

WHY I READ THIS BOOK

FAVORITE QUOTES

THINGS I LIKED

THINGS I DIDN'T LIKE

RECOMMEND THIS TO

TAGS/CATEGORY
(PLACE TO NOTE GOODREADS SHELF
OR BLOG POST CATEGORY)

FEELING, MOOD, TONE

BOOK TITLE [   ]   AUTHOR [   ]

GENRE   SERIES   SERIES #   PAGE COUNT/HOURS
[   ]   [   ]   [   ] [   ]

FORMAT:
EBOOK | PAPERBACK | AUDIOBOOK
LIBRARY BORROW | KINDLE UNLIMITED | OTHER

RATING ☆☆☆☆☆

DATE STARTED   DATE FINISHED
[   ]   [   ]   DID NOT FINISH [ ]

MAIN CHARACTER(S) [   ]

SUPPORTING CHARACTERS [   ]

SETTING [   ]

WHODUNIT [   ]

🕮 THOUGHTS ON THE PLOT/THEME 🕮

🕮 THOUGHTS ON MYSTERY 🕮

🕮 THOUGHTS ON CHARACTERS 🕮

Wrap up Section

WHY I READ THIS BOOK

FAVORITE QUOTES

THINGS I LIKED

THINGS I DIDN'T LIKE

RECOMMEND THIS TO

TAGS/CATEGORY
(PLACE TO NOTE GOODREADS SHELF
OR BLOG POST CATEGORY)

FEELING, MOOD, TONE

BOOK TITLE [   ]   AUTHOR [   ]

GENRE   SERIES   SERIES #   PAGE COUNT/HOURS
[   ]   [   ]   [   ]   [   ]

FORMAT:
EBOOK | PAPERBACK | AUDIOBOOK
LIBRARY BORROW | KINDLE UNLIMITED | OTHER

RATING ☆☆☆☆☆

DATE STARTED   DATE FINISHED
[   ]   [   ]   DID NOT FINISH [ ]

MAIN CHARACTER(S) [   ]

SUPPORTING CHARACTERS [   ]

SETTING [   ]

WHODUNIT [   ]

THOUGHTS ON THE PLOT/THEME

THOUGHTS ON MYSTERY

THOUGHTS ON CHARACTERS

Wrap up Section

WHY I READ THIS BOOK

FAVORITE QUOTES

THINGS I LIKED

THINGS I DIDN'T LIKE

RECOMMEND THIS TO

TAGS/CATEGORY
(PLACE TO NOTE GOODREADS SHELF
OR BLOG POST CATEGORY)

FEELING, MOOD, TONE 😃 😔 😍 😢 😂 😲

June

"Revenge is sweet and not fattening."
Alfred Hitchcock

June

Audiobook Appreciation Month

SUNDAY	MONDAY	TUESDAY	WEDNESDAY
			1
5	6	7	8
12	13	14	15
19	20	21	22
26	27	28	29

THURSDAY	FRIDAY	SATURDAY
2	3	4
9	10	11
16	17	18
23	24	25
30		

BOOK TITLE [   ] AUTHOR [   ]

GENRE   SERIES   SERIES #   PAGE COUNT/HOURS
[   ]   [   ]   [   ]   [   ]

FORMAT:
EBOOK | PAPERBACK | AUDIOBOOK   RATING ☆☆☆☆☆
LIBRARY BORROW | KINDLE UNLIMITED | OTHER

DATE STARTED   DATE FINISHED
[   ]   [   ]   DID NOT FINISH [   ]

MAIN CHARACTER(S) [   ]
SUPPORTING CHARACTERS [   ]
SETTING [   ]
WHODUNIT [   ]

THOUGHTS ON THE PLOT/THEME

THOUGHTS ON MYSTERY

THOUGHTS ON CHARACTERS

Wrap up Section

WHY I READ THIS BOOK

FAVORITE QUOTES

THINGS I LIKED

THINGS I DIDN'T LIKE

RECOMMEND THIS TO

TAGS/CATEGORY
(PLACE TO NOTE GOODREADS SHELF
OR BLOG POST CATEGORY)

FEELING, MOOD, TONE

BOOK TITLE [.   ]   AUTHOR [   ]

GENRE   SERIES   SERIES #   PAGE COUNT/HOURS
[   ]   [   ]   [   ]   [   ]

FORMAT:
EBOOK | PAPERBACK | AUDIOBOOK
LIBRARY BORROW | KINDLE UNLIMITED | OTHER

RATING ☆☆☆☆☆

DATE STARTED   DATE FINISHED
[   ]   [   ]   DID NOT FINISH [ ]

MAIN CHARACTER(S) [   ]

SUPPORTING CHARACTERS [   ]

SETTING [   ]

WHODUNIT [   ]

THOUGHTS ON THE PLOT/THEME

THOUGHTS ON MYSTERY

THOUGHTS ON CHARACTERS

Wrap up Section

WHY I READ THIS BOOK

FAVORITE QUOTES

THINGS I LIKED

THINGS I DIDN'T LIKE

RECOMMEND THIS TO

TAGS/CATEGORY
(PLACE TO NOTE GOODREADS SHELF
OR BLOG POST CATEGORY)

FEELING, MOOD, TONE 😃 😔 😍 😣 😂 😲

BOOK TITLE [   ]   **AUTHOR** [   ]

GENRE   **SERIES**   **SERIES #**   **PAGE COUNT/HOURS**
[   ]   [   ]   [   ]   [   ]

FORMAT:

EBOOK | PAPERBACK | AUDIOBOOK
LIBRARY BORROW | KINDLE UNLIMITED | OTHER

RATING ☆☆☆☆☆

DATE STARTED   **DATE FINISHED**
[   ]   [   ]   **DID NOT FINISH** [   ]

MAIN CHARACTER(S) [   ]

SUPPORTING CHARACTERS [   ]

SETTING [   ]

WHODUNIT [   ]

THOUGHTS ON THE PLOT/THEME

THOUGHTS ON MYSTERY

THOUGHTS ON CHARACTERS

Wrap up Section

WHY I READ THIS BOOK

FAVORITE QUOTES

THINGS I LIKED

THINGS I DIDN'T LIKE

RECOMMEND THIS TO

TAGS/CATEGORY
(PLACE TO NOTE GOODREADS SHELF
OR BLOG POST CATEGORY)

FEELING, MOOD, TONE

BOOK TITLE [   ] **AUTHOR** [   ]

GENRE   **SERIES**   **SERIES #** **PAGE COUNT/HOURS**
[   ]   [   ]   [   ]   [   ]

FORMAT:

EBOOK | PAPERBACK | AUDIOBOOK
LIBRARY BORROW | KINDLE UNLIMITED | OTHER

RATING ☆☆☆☆☆

DATE STARTED   **DATE FINISHED**
[   ]   [   ]   **DID NOT FINISH** [   ]

MAIN CHARACTER(S) [   ]

SUPPORTING CHARACTERS [   ]

SETTING [   ]

WHODUNIT [   ]

THOUGHTS ON THE PLOT/THEME

THOUGHTS ON MYSTERY

THOUGHTS ON CHARACTERS

Wrap up Section

WHY I READ THIS BOOK

FAVORITE QUOTES

THINGS I LIKED

THINGS I DIDN'T LIKE

RECOMMEND THIS TO

TAGS/CATEGORY
(PLACE TO NOTE GOODREADS SHELF
OR BLOG POST CATEGORY)

FEELING, MOOD, TONE

BOOK TITLE [   ] AUTHOR [   ]

GENRE   SERIES   SERIES # PAGE COUNT/HOURS
[   ]   [   ]   [   ]   [   ]

FORMAT:

EBOOK | PAPERBACK | AUDIOBOOK   RATING ☆☆☆☆☆
LIBRARY BORROW | KINDLE UNLIMITED | OTHER

DATE STARTED   DATE FINISHED
[   ]   [   ]   DID NOT FINISH [   ]

MAIN CHARACTER(S) [   ]

SUPPORTING CHARACTERS [   ]

SETTING [   ]

WHODUNIT [   ]

THOUGHTS ON THE PLOT/THEME

THOUGHTS ON MYSTERY

THOUGHTS ON CHARACTERS

Wrap up Section

WHY I READ THIS BOOK

FAVORITE QUOTES

THINGS I LIKED

THINGS I DIDN'T LIKE

RECOMMEND THIS TO

TAGS/CATEGORY
{PLACE TO NOTE GOODREADS SHELF
OR BLOG POST CATEGORY}

FEELING, MOOD, TONE

July

"Conversations are always dangerous,
if you have something to hide."
A Caribbean Mystery by Agatha Christie

July

SUNDAY	MONDAY	TUESDAY	WEDNESDAY
31			
3	4	5	6
10	11	12	13
17	18	19	20
24	25	26	27

THURSDAY	FRIDAY	SATURDAY
	1	2
7	8	9
14	15	16
21	22	23
28	29	30

BOOK TITLE _____ AUTHOR _____

GENRE _____ SERIES _____ SERIES # ____ PAGE COUNT/HOURS _____

FORMAT:

EBOOK | PAPERBACK | AUDIOBOOK
LIBRARY BORROW | KINDLE UNLIMITED | OTHER

RATING ☆☆☆☆☆

DATE STARTED _____ DATE FINISHED _____ DID NOT FINISH ☐

MAIN CHARACTER(S) _____

SUPPORTING CHARACTERS _____

SETTING _____

WHODUNIT _____

THOUGHTS ON THE PLOT/THEME

THOUGHTS ON MYSTERY

THOUGHTS ON CHARACTERS

Wrap up Section

WHY I READ THIS BOOK

FAVORITE QUOTES

THINGS I LIKED

THINGS I DIDN'T LIKE

RECOMMEND THIS TO

TAGS/CATEGORY
{PLACE TO NOTE GOODREADS SHELF
OR BLOG POST CATEGORY}

FEELING, MOOD, TONE

BOOK TITLE [ ] AUTHOR [ ]

GENRE SERIES SERIES # PAGE COUNT/HOURS
[ ] [ ] [ ] [ ]

FORMAT:

EBOOK | PAPERBACK | AUDIOBOOK
LIBRARY BORROW | KINDLE UNLIMITED | OTHER

RATING ☆☆☆☆☆

DATE STARTED DATE FINISHED
[ ] [ ] DID NOT FINISH [ ]

MAIN CHARACTER(S) [ ]

SUPPORTING CHARACTERS [ ]

SETTING [ ]

WHODUNIT [ ]

THOUGHTS ON THE PLOT/THEME

THOUGHTS ON MYSTERY

THOUGHTS ON CHARACTERS

Wrap up Section

WHY I READ THIS BOOK

FAVORITE QUOTES

THINGS I LIKED

THINGS I DIDN'T LIKE

RECOMMEND THIS TO

TAGS/CATEGORY
(PLACE TO NOTE GOODREADS SHELF
OR BLOG POST CATEGORY)

FEELING, MOOD, TONE

BOOK TITLE [   ] AUTHOR [   ]

GENRE   SERIES   SERIES #   PAGE COUNT/HOURS
[   ]   [   ]   [   ]   [   ]

FORMAT:
EBOOK | PAPERBACK | AUDIOBOOK
LIBRARY BORROW | KINDLE UNLIMITED | OTHER

RATING ☆☆☆☆☆

DATE STARTED   DATE FINISHED
[   ]   [   ]   DID NOT FINISH [ ]

MAIN CHARACTER(S) [   ]

SUPPORTING CHARACTERS [   ]

SETTING [   ]

WHODUNIT [   ]

THOUGHTS ON THE PLOT/THEME

THOUGHTS ON MYSTERY

THOUGHTS ON CHARACTERS

Wrap up Section

WHY I READ THIS BOOK

FAVORITE QUOTES

THINGS I LIKED

THINGS I DIDN'T LIKE

RECOMMEND THIS TO

TAGS/CATEGORY
(PLACE TO NOTE GOODREADS SHELF
OR BLOG POST CATEGORY)

FEELING, MOOD, TONE 😃 😔 😍 😣 😂 😲

BOOK TITLE [   ] AUTHOR [   ]

GENRE   SERIES   SERIES #   PAGE COUNT/HOURS
[   ]   [   ]   [   ]   [   ]

FORMAT:

EBOOK | PAPERBACK | AUDIOBOOK
LIBRARY BORROW | KINDLE UNLIMITED | OTHER

RATING ☆☆☆☆☆

DATE STARTED   DATE FINISHED
[   ]   [   ]   DID NOT FINISH [ ]

MAIN CHARACTER(S) [   ]

SUPPORTING CHARACTERS [   ]

SETTING [   ]

WHODUNIT [   ]

THOUGHTS ON THE PLOT/THEME

THOUGHTS ON MYSTERY

THOUGHTS ON CHARACTERS

Wrap up Section

WHY I READ THIS BOOK

FAVORITE QUOTES

THINGS I LIKED

THINGS I DIDN'T LIKE

RECOMMEND THIS TO

TAGS/CATEGORY
(PLACE TO NOTE GOODREADS SHELF
OR BLOG POST CATEGORY)

FEELING, MOOD, TONE

BOOK TITLE [   ]   AUTHOR [   ]

GENRE   SERIES   SERIES #   PAGE COUNT/HOURS
[   ]   [   ]   [   ]   [   ]

FORMAT:
EBOOK | PAPERBACK | AUDIOBOOK
LIBRARY BORROW | KINDLE UNLIMITED | OTHER

RATING ☆☆☆☆☆

DATE STARTED   DATE FINISHED
[   ]   [   ]   DID NOT FINISH [ ]

MAIN CHARACTER(S) [   ]

SUPPORTING CHARACTERS [   ]

SETTING [   ]

WHODUNIT [   ]

THOUGHTS ON THE PLOT/THEME

THOUGHTS ON MYSTERY

THOUGHTS ON CHARACTERS

Wrap up Section

WHY I READ THIS BOOK

FAVORITE QUOTES

THINGS I LIKED

THINGS I DIDN'T LIKE

RECOMMEND THIS TO

TAGS/CATEGORY
(PLACE TO NOTE GOODREADS SHELF
OR BLOG POST CATEGORY)

FEELING, MOOD, TONE

August

"People are straightforward enough,
on the whole, till one starts to look for crooked motives,
and then, oh boy, how crooked can they be!"

The Ivy Tree by Mary Stewart

August

This Month is Read a Romance Month

SUNDAY	MONDAY	TUESDAY	WEDNESDAY
	1	2	3
7	8	9	10
14	15	16	17
21	22	23	24
28	29	30	31

THURSDAY	FRIDAY	SATURDAY
4	5	6
11	12	13
18	19	20
25	26	27

BOOK TITLE [   ] AUTHOR [   ]

GENRE   SERIES   SERIES #   PAGE COUNT/HOURS
[   ]   [   ]   [   ]   [   ]

FORMAT:

EBOOK | PAPERBACK | AUDIOBOOK
LIBRARY BORROW | KINDLE UNLIMITED | OTHER

RATING ☆☆☆☆☆

DATE STARTED   DATE FINISHED
[   ]   [   ]   DID NOT FINISH [ ]

MAIN CHARACTER(S) [   ]

SUPPORTING CHARACTERS [   ]

SETTING [   ]

WHODUNIT [   ]

THOUGHTS ON THE PLOT/THEME

THOUGHTS ON MYSTERY

THOUGHTS ON CHARACTERS

Wrap up Section

WHY I READ THIS BOOK

FAVORITE QUOTES

THINGS I LIKED

THINGS I DIDN'T LIKE

RECOMMEND THIS TO

TAGS/CATEGORY
(PLACE TO NOTE GOODREADS SHELF
OR BLOG POST CATEGORY)

FEELING, MOOD, TONE

BOOK TITLE [   ] **AUTHOR** [   ]

GENRE   **SERIES**   **SERIES #** **PAGE COUNT/HOURS**
[   ]   [   ]   [   ]   [   ]

FORMAT:

EBOOK | PAPERBACK | AUDIOBOOK
LIBRARY BORROW | KINDLE UNLIMITED | OTHER

RATING ☆☆☆☆☆

DATE STARTED   **DATE FINISHED**
[   ]   [   ]   **DID NOT FINISH** [ ]

MAIN CHARACTER(S) [   ]

SUPPORTING CHARACTERS [   ]

SETTING [   ]

WHODUNIT [   ]

THOUGHTS ON THE PLOT/THEME

THOUGHTS ON MYSTERY

THOUGHTS ON CHARACTERS

Wrap up Section

WHY I READ THIS BOOK

FAVORITE QUOTES

THINGS I LIKED

THINGS I DIDN'T LIKE

RECOMMEND THIS TO

TAGS/CATEGORY
(PLACE TO NOTE GOODREADS SHELF
OR BLOG POST CATEGORY)

FEELING, MOOD, TONE 😃 😔 😍 😰 😂 😲

BOOK TITLE [   ] AUTHOR [   ]

GENRE [   ] SERIES [   ] SERIES # [   ] PAGE COUNT/HOURS [   ]

FORMAT:

EBOOK | PAPERBACK | AUDIOBOOK
LIBRARY BORROW | KINDLE UNLIMITED | OTHER

RATING ☆☆☆☆☆

DATE STARTED [   ] DATE FINISHED [   ] DID NOT FINISH [   ]

MAIN CHARACTER(S) [   ]

SUPPORTING CHARACTERS [   ]

SETTING [   ]

WHODUNIT [   ]

THOUGHTS ON THE PLOT/THEME

THOUGHTS ON MYSTERY

THOUGHTS ON CHARACTERS

Wrap up Section

WHY I READ THIS BOOK

FAVORITE QUOTES

THINGS I LIKED

THINGS I DIDN'T LIKE

RECOMMEND THIS TO

TAGS/CATEGORY
{PLACE TO NOTE GOODREADS SHELF
OR BLOG POST CATEGORY}

FEELING, MOOD, TONE 😃 😔 😍 😣 😂 😲

BOOK TITLE [   ]   AUTHOR [   ]

GENRE   SERIES   SERIES #   PAGE COUNT/HOURS
[   ]   [   ]   [   ]   [   ]

FORMAT:
EBOOK | PAPERBACK | AUDIOBOOK   RATING ☆☆☆☆☆
LIBRARY BORROW | KINDLE UNLIMITED | OTHER

DATE STARTED   DATE FINISHED
[   ]   [   ]   DID NOT FINISH [ ]

MAIN CHARACTER(S) [   ]
SUPPORTING CHARACTERS [   ]
SETTING [   ]
WHODUNIT [   ]

THOUGHTS ON THE PLOT/THEME

THOUGHTS ON MYSTERY

THOUGHTS ON CHARACTERS

Wrap up Section

WHY I READ THIS BOOK

FAVORITE QUOTES

THINGS I LIKED

THINGS I DIDN'T LIKE

RECOMMEND THIS TO

TAGS/CATEGORY
(PLACE TO NOTE GOODREADS SHELF
OR BLOG POST CATEGORY)

FEELING, MOOD, TONE

BOOK TITLE [   ]   AUTHOR [   ]

GENRE   SERIES   SERIES #   PAGE COUNT/HOURS
[   ]   [   ]   [   ]   [   ]

FORMAT:
EBOOK | PAPERBACK | AUDIOBOOK
LIBRARY BORROW | KINDLE UNLIMITED | OTHER

RATING ☆☆☆☆☆

DATE STARTED   DATE FINISHED
[   ]   [   ]   DID NOT FINISH [   ]

MAIN CHARACTER(S) [   ]

SUPPORTING CHARACTERS [   ]

SETTING [   ]

WHODUNIT [   ]

THOUGHTS ON THE PLOT/THEME

THOUGHTS ON MYSTERY

THOUGHTS ON CHARACTERS

Wrap up Section

WHY I READ THIS BOOK

FAVORITE QUOTES

THINGS I LIKED

THINGS I DIDN'T LIKE

RECOMMEND THIS TO

TAGS/CATEGORY
(PLACE TO NOTE GOODREADS SHELF
OR BLOG POST CATEGORY)

FEELING, MOOD, TONE

September

"Truth will come to sight; murder cannot be hid long."
The Merchant of Venice by William Shakespeare

Library Card Sign-up Month

SUNDAY	MONDAY	TUESDAY	WEDNESDAY
4	5	6	7
11	12	13	14
18	19	20	21
25	26	27	28

BOOKISH DATES OF THE MONTH

4 - Cyril Hare's birthday
6 - Read a Book Day
10 - Peter Lovesey's birthday
15 - Cozy Mystery Day
     (Agatha Christie's birthday)
29 - Historical Mystery Day
     (Elizabeth Peters' birthday)

THURSDAY	FRIDAY	SATURDAY
1	2	3
8	9	10
15	16	17
22	23	24
29	30	

133

BOOK TITLE [   ]   AUTHOR [   ]

GENRE   SERIES   SERIES #   PAGE COUNT/HOURS
[   ]   [   ]   [   ]   [   ]

FORMAT:
EBOOK | PAPERBACK | AUDIOBOOK   RATING ☆☆☆☆☆
LIBRARY BORROW | KINDLE UNLIMITED | OTHER

DATE STARTED   DATE FINISHED
[   ]   [   ]   DID NOT FINISH [   ]

MAIN CHARACTER(S) [   ]

SUPPORTING CHARACTERS [   ]

SETTING [   ]

WHODUNIT [   ]

THOUGHTS ON THE PLOT/THEME

THOUGHTS ON MYSTERY

THOUGHTS ON CHARACTERS

Wrap up Section

WHY I READ THIS BOOK

FAVORITE QUOTES

THINGS I LIKED

THINGS I DIDN'T LIKE

RECOMMEND THIS TO

TAGS/CATEGORY
(PLACE TO NOTE GOODREADS SHELF
OR BLOG POST CATEGORY)

FEELING, MOOD, TONE

BOOK TITLE [   ] AUTHOR [   ]

GENRE   SERIES   SERIES #   PAGE COUNT/HOURS
[   ]   [   ]   [   ]   [   ]

FORMAT:
EBOOK | PAPERBACK | AUDIOBOOK
LIBRARY BORROW | KINDLE UNLIMITED | OTHER

RATING ☆☆☆☆☆

DATE STARTED   DATE FINISHED
[   ]   [   ]   DID NOT FINISH [   ]

MAIN CHARACTER(S) [   ]

SUPPORTING CHARACTERS [   ]

SETTING [   ]

WHODUNIT [   ]

THOUGHTS ON THE PLOT/THEME

THOUGHTS ON MYSTERY

THOUGHTS ON CHARACTERS

Wrap up Section

WHY I READ THIS BOOK

FAVORITE QUOTES

THINGS I LIKED

THINGS I DIDN'T LIKE

RECOMMEND THIS TO

TAGS/CATEGORY
(PLACE TO NOTE GOODREADS SHELF
OR BLOG POST CATEGORY)

FEELING, MOOD, TONE 😃 😔 😍 😣 😂 😲

BOOK TITLE [   ] AUTHOR [   ]

GENRE [   ] SERIES [   ] SERIES # [   ] PAGE COUNT/HOURS [   ]

FORMAT:

EBOOK | PAPERBACK | AUDIOBOOK
LIBRARY BORROW | KINDLE UNLIMITED | OTHER

RATING ☆☆☆☆☆

DATE STARTED [   ] DATE FINISHED [   ] DID NOT FINISH [   ]

MAIN CHARACTER(S) [   ]

SUPPORTING CHARACTERS [   ]

SETTING [   ]

WHODUNIT [   ]

THOUGHTS ON THE PLOT/THEME

THOUGHTS ON MYSTERY

THOUGHTS ON CHARACTERS

Wrap up Section

WHY I READ THIS BOOK

FAVORITE QUOTES

THINGS I LIKED

THINGS I DIDN'T LIKE

RECOMMEND THIS TO

TAGS/CATEGORY
(PLACE TO NOTE GOODREADS SHELF
OR BLOG POST CATEGORY)

FEELING, MOOD, TONE

BOOK TITLE _____ AUTHOR _____

GENRE   SERIES   SERIES #   PAGE COUNT/HOURS
_____   _____   _____   _____

FORMAT:
EBOOK | PAPERBACK | AUDIOBOOK
LIBRARY BORROW | KINDLE UNLIMITED | OTHER

RATING ☆☆☆☆☆

DATE STARTED   DATE FINISHED
_____   _____   DID NOT FINISH ☐

MAIN CHARACTER(S) _____

SUPPORTING CHARACTERS _____

SETTING _____

WHODUNIT _____

THOUGHTS ON THE PLOT/THEME

THOUGHTS ON MYSTERY

THOUGHTS ON CHARACTERS

Wrap up Section

WHY I READ THIS BOOK

FAVORITE QUOTES

THINGS I LIKED

THINGS I DIDN'T LIKE

RECOMMEND THIS TO

TAGS/CATEGORY
(PLACE TO NOTE GOODREADS SHELF
OR BLOG POST CATEGORY)

FEELING, MOOD, TONE 😃 😔 😍 😟 😆 😲

BOOK TITLE ☐   **AUTHOR** ☐

GENRE   **SERIES**   **SERIES #**   **PAGE COUNT/HOURS**

☐   ☐   ☐   ☐

FORMAT:

EBOOK | PAPERBACK | AUDIOBOOK
LIBRARY BORROW | KINDLE UNLIMITED | OTHER

RATING ☆☆☆☆☆

DATE STARTED   **DATE FINISHED**

☐   ☐   **DID NOT FINISH** ☐

MAIN CHARACTER(S) ☐

SUPPORTING CHARACTERS ☐

SETTING ☐

WHODUNIT ☐

THOUGHTS ON THE PLOT/THEME

THOUGHTS ON MYSTERY

THOUGHTS ON CHARACTERS

Wrap up Section

WHY I READ THIS BOOK

FAVORITE QUOTES

THINGS I LIKED

THINGS I DIDN'T LIKE

RECOMMEND THIS TO

TAGS/CATEGORY
(PLACE TO NOTE GOODREADS SHELF
OR BLOG POST CATEGORY)

FEELING, MOOD, TONE

October

"There simply must be a corpse in a detective novel,
and the deader the corpse the better."

S.S. Van Dine

First Full Week of October - Mystery Series Week

SUNDAY	MONDAY	TUESDAY	WEDNESDAY
30	31		
2	3	4	5
9	10	11	12
16	17	18	19
23	24	25	26

THURSDAY	FRIDAY	SATURDAY
		1
6	7	8
13	14	15
20	21	22
27	28	29

BOOK TITLE [   ] AUTHOR [   ]

GENRE   SERIES   SERIES #   PAGE COUNT/HOURS
[   ]   [   ]   [   ]   [   ]

FORMAT:
EBOOK | PAPERBACK | AUDIOBOOK
LIBRARY BORROW | KINDLE UNLIMITED | OTHER

RATING ☆☆☆☆☆

DATE STARTED   DATE FINISHED
[   ]   [   ]   DID NOT FINISH [ ]

MAIN CHARACTER(S) [   ]

SUPPORTING CHARACTERS [   ]

SETTING [   ]

WHODUNIT [   ]

THOUGHTS ON THE PLOT/THEME

THOUGHTS ON MYSTERY

THOUGHTS ON CHARACTERS

Wrap up Section

WHY I READ THIS BOOK

FAVORITE QUOTES

THINGS I LIKED

THINGS I DIDN'T LIKE

RECOMMEND THIS TO

TAGS/CATEGORY
(PLACE TO NOTE GOODREADS SHELF
OR BLOG POST CATEGORY)

FEELING, MOOD, TONE

BOOK TITLE [   ]   AUTHOR [   ]

GENRE   SERIES   SERIES #   PAGE COUNT/HOURS
[   ]   [   ]   [   ]   [   ]

FORMAT:

EBOOK | PAPERBACK | AUDIOBOOK   RATING ☆☆☆☆☆
LIBRARY BORROW | KINDLE UNLIMITED | OTHER

DATE STARTED   DATE FINISHED
[   ]   [   ]   DID NOT FINISH [ ]

MAIN CHARACTER(S) [   ]

SUPPORTING CHARACTERS [   ]

SETTING [   ]

WHODUNIT [   ]

THOUGHTS ON THE PLOT/THEME

THOUGHTS ON MYSTERY

THOUGHTS ON CHARACTERS

Wrap up Section

WHY I READ THIS BOOK

FAVORITE QUOTES

THINGS I LIKED

THINGS I DIDN'T LIKE

RECOMMEND THIS TO

TAGS/CATEGORY
{PLACE TO NOTE GOODREADS SHELF
OR BLOG POST CATEGORY}

FEELING, MOOD, TONE

BOOK TITLE [   ] AUTHOR [   ]

GENRE [   ] SERIES [   ] SERIES # [   ] PAGE COUNT/HOURS [   ]

FORMAT:

EBOOK | PAPERBACK | AUDIOBOOK
LIBRARY BORROW | KINDLE UNLIMITED | OTHER

RATING ☆☆☆☆☆

DATE STARTED [   ] DATE FINISHED [   ] DID NOT FINISH [   ]

MAIN CHARACTER(S) [   ]

SUPPORTING CHARACTERS [   ]

SETTING [   ]

WHODUNIT [   ]

THOUGHTS ON THE PLOT/THEME

THOUGHTS ON MYSTERY

THOUGHTS ON CHARACTERS

Wrap up Section

WHY I READ THIS BOOK

FAVORITE QUOTES

THINGS I LIKED

THINGS I DIDN'T LIKE

RECOMMEND THIS TO

TAGS/CATEGORY
(PLACE TO NOTE GOODREADS SHELF
OR BLOG POST CATEGORY)

FEELING, MOOD, TONE

BOOK TITLE _____ **AUTHOR** _____

GENRE _____ **SERIES** _____ **SERIES #** _____ **PAGE COUNT/HOURS** _____

FORMAT:
EBOOK | PAPERBACK | AUDIOBOOK
LIBRARY BORROW | KINDLE UNLIMITED | OTHER

RATING ☆☆☆☆☆

DATE STARTED _____ **DATE FINISHED** _____ **DID NOT FINISH** ☐

MAIN CHARACTER(S) _____

SUPPORTING CHARACTERS _____

SETTING _____

WHODUNIT _____

THOUGHTS ON THE PLOT/THEME

THOUGHTS ON MYSTERY

THOUGHTS ON CHARACTERS

Wrap up Section

WHY I READ THIS BOOK

FAVORITE QUOTES

THINGS I LIKED

THINGS I DIDN'T LIKE

RECOMMEND THIS TO

TAGS/CATEGORY
(PLACE TO NOTE GOODREADS SHELF
OR BLOG POST CATEGORY)

FEELING, MOOD, TONE

BOOK TITLE [   ]   AUTHOR [   ]

GENRE   SERIES   SERIES #   PAGE COUNT/HOURS
[   ]   [   ]   [   ]   [   ]

FORMAT:
EBOOK | PAPERBACK | AUDIOBOOK
LIBRARY BORROW | KINDLE UNLIMITED | OTHER

RATING ☆☆☆☆☆

DATE STARTED   DATE FINISHED
[   ]   [   ]   DID NOT FINISH [ ]

MAIN CHARACTER(S) [   ]

SUPPORTING CHARACTERS [   ]

SETTING [   ]

WHODUNIT [   ]

THOUGHTS ON THE PLOT/THEME

THOUGHTS ON MYSTERY

THOUGHTS ON CHARACTERS

Wrap up Section

WHY I READ THIS BOOK

FAVORITE QUOTES

THINGS I LIKED

THINGS I DIDN'T LIKE

RECOMMEND THIS TO

TAGS/CATEGORY
{PLACE TO NOTE GOODREADS SHELF
OR BLOG POST CATEGORY}

FEELING, MOOD, TONE

November

"The great advantage about telling
the truth is that nobody ever believes it."
Dorothy L. Sayers

November

National Novel Writing Month

SUNDAY	MONDAY	TUESDAY	WEDNESDAY
		1	2
6	7	8	9
13	14	15	16
20	21	22	23
27	28	29	30

THURSDAY	FRIDAY	SATURDAY
3	4	5
10	11	12
17	18	19
24	25	26

BOOK TITLE [   ]   AUTHOR [   ]

GENRE   SERIES   SERIES #   PAGE COUNT/HOURS
[   ]   [   ]   [   ]   [   ]

FORMAT:
EBOOK | PAPERBACK | AUDIOBOOK
LIBRARY BORROW | KINDLE UNLIMITED | OTHER

RATING ☆☆☆☆☆

DATE STARTED   DATE FINISHED
[   ]   [   ]   DID NOT FINISH [ ]

MAIN CHARACTER(S) [   ]

SUPPORTING CHARACTERS [   ]

SETTING [   ]

WHODUNIT [   ]

THOUGHTS ON THE PLOT/THEME

THOUGHTS ON MYSTERY

THOUGHTS ON CHARACTERS

Wrap up Section

WHY I READ THIS BOOK

FAVORITE QUOTES

THINGS I LIKED

THINGS I DIDN'T LIKE

RECOMMEND THIS TO

TAGS/CATEGORY
(PLACE TO NOTE GOODREADS SHELF
OR BLOG POST CATEGORY)

FEELING, MOOD, TONE 😃 😔 😍 😟 😂 😲

BOOK TITLE [   ] AUTHOR [   ]

GENRE [   ] SERIES [   ] SERIES # [   ] PAGE COUNT/HOURS [   ]

FORMAT:
EBOOK | PAPERBACK | AUDIOBOOK
LIBRARY BORROW | KINDLE UNLIMITED | OTHER

RATING ☆☆☆☆☆

DATE STARTED [   ] DATE FINISHED [   ] DID NOT FINISH [   ]

MAIN CHARACTER(S) [   ]

SUPPORTING CHARACTERS [   ]

SETTING [   ]

WHODUNIT [   ]

THOUGHTS ON THE PLOT/THEME

THOUGHTS ON MYSTERY

THOUGHTS ON CHARACTERS

Wrap up Section

WHY I READ THIS BOOK

FAVORITE QUOTES

THINGS I LIKED

THINGS I DIDN'T LIKE

RECOMMEND THIS TO

TAGS/CATEGORY
(PLACE TO NOTE GOODREADS SHELF
OR BLOG POST CATEGORY)

FEELING, MOOD, TONE

BOOK TITLE _____   **AUTHOR** _____

GENRE   **SERIES**   **SERIES #**   **PAGE COUNT/HOURS**
_____   _____   ____   _____

FORMAT:

EBOOK | PAPERBACK | AUDIOBOOK
LIBRARY BORROW | KINDLE UNLIMITED | OTHER

RATING ☆☆☆☆☆

DATE STARTED   **DATE FINISHED**
_____   _____   **DID NOT FINISH** ☐

MAIN CHARACTER(S) _____

SUPPORTING CHARACTERS _____

SETTING _____

WHODUNIT _____

THOUGHTS ON THE PLOT/THEME

THOUGHTS ON MYSTERY

THOUGHTS ON CHARACTERS

Wrap up Section

WHY I READ THIS BOOK

FAVORITE QUOTES

THINGS I LIKED

THINGS I DIDN'T LIKE

RECOMMEND THIS TO

TAGS/CATEGORY
(PLACE TO NOTE GOODREADS SHELF
OR BLOG POST CATEGORY)

FEELING, MOOD, TONE

BOOK TITLE [   ]   AUTHOR [   ]

GENRE   SERIES   SERIES #   PAGE COUNT/HOURS
[   ]   [   ]   [   ] [   ]

FORMAT:

EBOOK | PAPERBACK | AUDIOBOOK
LIBRARY BORROW | KINDLE UNLIMITED | OTHER

RATING ☆☆☆☆☆

DATE STARTED   DATE FINISHED
[   ]   [   ]   DID NOT FINISH [ ]

MAIN CHARACTER(S) [   ]

SUPPORTING CHARACTERS [   ]

SETTING [   ]

WHODUNIT [   ]

THOUGHTS ON THE PLOT/THEME

THOUGHTS ON MYSTERY

THOUGHTS ON CHARACTERS

Wrap up Section

WHY I READ THIS BOOK

FAVORITE QUOTES

THINGS I LIKED

THINGS I DIDN'T LIKE

RECOMMEND THIS TO

TAGS/CATEGORY
(PLACE TO NOTE GOODREADS SHELF
OR BLOG POST CATEGORY)

FEELING, MOOD, TONE

BOOK TITLE [_____] **AUTHOR** [_____]

GENRE **SERIES** **SERIES #** **PAGE COUNT/HOURS**
[_____] [_____] [____] [_____]

FORMAT:

EBOOK | PAPERBACK | AUDIOBOOK
LIBRARY BORROW | KINDLE UNLIMITED | OTHER

RATING ☆☆☆☆☆

DATE STARTED **DATE FINISHED**
[_____] [_____] **DID NOT FINISH** [__]

MAIN CHARACTER(S) [_____]

SUPPORTING CHARACTERS [_____]

SETTING [_____]

WHODUNIT [_____]

THOUGHTS ON THE PLOT/THEME

THOUGHTS ON MYSTERY

THOUGHTS ON CHARACTERS

Wrap up Section

WHY I READ THIS BOOK

FAVORITE QUOTES

THINGS I LIKED

THINGS I DIDN'T LIKE

RECOMMEND THIS TO

TAGS/CATEGORY
(PLACE TO NOTE GOODREADS SHELF
OR BLOG POST CATEGORY)

FEELING, MOOD, TONE

December

"Very few of us are what we seem."

The Man in the Mist by Agatha Christie

December

Read a New Book Month

SUNDAY	MONDAY	TUESDAY	WEDNESDAY
4	5	6	7
11	12	13	14
18	19	20	21
25	26	27	28

THURSDAY	FRIDAY	SATURDAY
1	2	3
8	9	10
15	16	17
22	23	24
29	30	31

BOOK TITLE [   ] AUTHOR [   ]

GENRE [   ] SERIES [   ] SERIES # [   ] PAGE COUNT/HOURS [   ]

FORMAT:

EBOOK | PAPERBACK | AUDIOBOOK
LIBRARY BORROW | KINDLE UNLIMITED | OTHER

RATING ☆☆☆☆☆

DATE STARTED [   ] DATE FINISHED [   ] DID NOT FINISH [   ]

MAIN CHARACTER(S) [   ]

SUPPORTING CHARACTERS [   ]

SETTING [   ]

WHODUNIT [   ]

THOUGHTS ON THE PLOT/THEME

THOUGHTS ON MYSTERY

THOUGHTS ON CHARACTERS

Wrap up Section

WHY I READ THIS BOOK

FAVORITE QUOTES

THINGS I LIKED

THINGS I DIDN'T LIKE

RECOMMEND THIS TO

TAGS/CATEGORY
(PLACE TO NOTE GOODREADS SHELF
OR BLOG POST CATEGORY)

FEELING, MOOD, TONE

BOOK TITLE [　　　　　　　　　]　　AUTHOR [　　　　　　　　]

GENRE　　　　　　　SERIES　　　　　　SERIES #　PAGE COUNT/HOURS
[　　　　　　]　　[　　　　　　]　　[　　]　　[　　　　　]

FORMAT:

EBOOK | PAPERBACK | AUDIOBOOK　　　RATING ☆☆☆☆☆
LIBRARY BORROW | KINDLE UNLIMITED | OTHER

DATE STARTED　　DATE FINISHED
[　　　　　]　　[　　　　　]　　DID NOT FINISH [　]

MAIN CHARACTER(S) [　　　　　　　　　　　　　]

SUPPORTING CHARACTERS [　　　　　　　　　　]

SETTING [　　　　　　　　　　　　　　　　]

WHODUNIT [　　　　　　　　　　　　　　　]

THOUGHTS ON THE PLOT/THEME

THOUGHTS ON MYSTERY

THOUGHTS ON CHARACTERS

Wrap up Section

WHY I READ THIS BOOK

FAVORITE QUOTES

THINGS I LIKED

THINGS I DIDN'T LIKE

RECOMMEND THIS TO

TAGS/CATEGORY
{PLACE TO NOTE GOODREADS SHELF
OR BLOG POST CATEGORY}

FEELING, MOOD, TONE

BOOK TITLE [   ]   AUTHOR [   ]

GENRE   SERIES   SERIES #   PAGE COUNT/HOURS
[   ]   [   ]   [   ]   [   ]

FORMAT:
EBOOK | PAPERBACK | AUDIOBOOK
LIBRARY BORROW | KINDLE UNLIMITED | OTHER

RATING ☆☆☆☆☆

DATE STARTED   DATE FINISHED
[   ]   [   ]   DID NOT FINISH [ ]

MAIN CHARACTER(S) [   ]

SUPPORTING CHARACTERS [   ]

SETTING [   ]

WHODUNIT [   ]

THOUGHTS ON THE PLOT/THEME

THOUGHTS ON MYSTERY

THOUGHTS ON CHARACTERS

Wrap up Section

WHY I READ THIS BOOK

FAVORITE QUOTES

THINGS I LIKED

THINGS I DIDN'T LIKE

RECOMMEND THIS TO

TAGS/CATEGORY
[PLACE TO NOTE GOODREADS SHELF
OR BLOG POST CATEGORY]

FEELING, MOOD, TONE

BOOK TITLE [   ]   AUTHOR [   ]

GENRE   SERIES   SERIES #   PAGE COUNT/HOURS
[   ]   [   ]   [   ]   [   ]

FORMAT:
EBOOK | PAPERBACK | AUDIOBOOK
LIBRARY BORROW | KINDLE UNLIMITED | OTHER

RATING ☆☆☆☆☆

DATE STARTED   DATE FINISHED
[   ]   [   ]   DID NOT FINISH [ ]

MAIN CHARACTER(S) [   ]

SUPPORTING CHARACTERS [   ]

SETTING [   ]

WHODUNIT [   ]

THOUGHTS ON THE PLOT/THEME

THOUGHTS ON MYSTERY

THOUGHTS ON CHARACTERS

Wrap up Section

WHY I READ THIS BOOK

FAVORITE QUOTES

THINGS I LIKED

THINGS I DIDN'T LIKE

RECOMMEND THIS TO

TAGS/CATEGORY
(PLACE TO NOTE GOODREADS SHELF
OR BLOG POST CATEGORY)

FEELING, MOOD, TONE

BOOK TITLE [   ]   **AUTHOR** [   ]

GENRE   **SERIES**   **SERIES #**   **PAGE COUNT/HOURS**
[   ]   [   ]   [   ]   [   ]

FORMAT:

EBOOK | PAPERBACK | AUDIOBOOK
LIBRARY BORROW | KINDLE UNLIMITED | OTHER

RATING ☆☆☆☆☆

DATE STARTED   **DATE FINISHED**
[   ]   [   ]   **DID NOT FINISH** [   ]

MAIN CHARACTER(S) [   ]

SUPPORTING CHARACTERS [   ]

SETTING [   ]

WHODUNIT [   ]

THOUGHTS ON THE PLOT/THEME

THOUGHTS ON MYSTERY

THOUGHTS ON CHARACTERS

Wrap up Section

WHY I READ THIS BOOK

FAVORITE QUOTES

THINGS I LIKED

THINGS I DIDN'T LIKE

RECOMMEND THIS TO

TAGS/CATEGORY
{PLACE TO NOTE GOODREADS SHELF
OR BLOG POST CATEGORY}

FEELING, MOOD, TONE

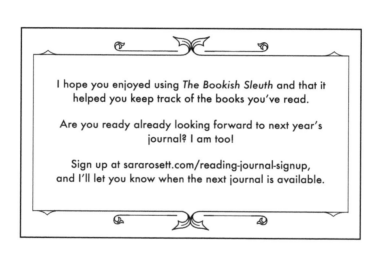

I hope you enjoyed using *The Bookish Sleuth* and that it helped you keep track of the books you've read.

Are you ready already looking forward to next year's journal? I am too!

Sign up at sararosett.com/reading-journal-signup, and I'll let you know when the next journal is available.

CPSIA information can be obtained
at www.ICGtesting.com
Printed in the USA
LVHW091337120322
713310LV00002B/118